S0-AIB-095

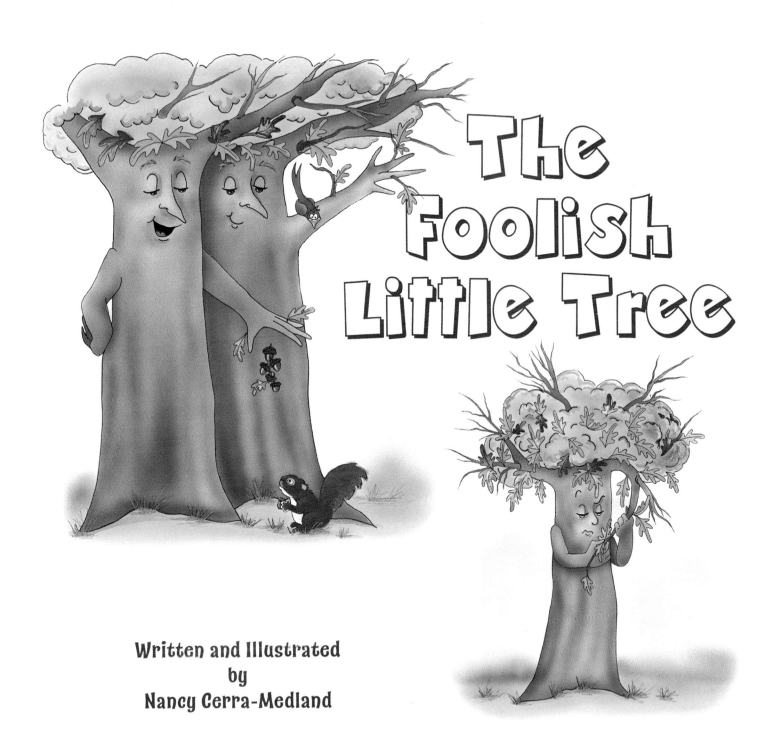

The Foolish Little Tree

Written and Illustrated
by
Nancy Cerra-Medland

Text and Illustrations copyright   2017 l© Nancy Cerra-Medland

All rights reserved. No part of this publication may be reproduced, or stored in a retrieval system, or

transmitted in any form or by any means, electronic, mechanical, photocopying, recording, or

otherwise, without written permission of the publisher.

LIBRARY OF CONGRESS CATALOGING - IN - PUBLICATION DATA

Cerra-Medland, Nancy

The foolish little tree / written and illustrated by Nancy Cerra-Medland.-1st ed.   p. cm.

Summary: Little tree faces her first change of seasons in her forest home. With the help of her friend

the caterpillar, she overcomes her fears and discovers that change isn't so scary.

ISBN: 978-1-48359-397-5

[1. Plant adaptation-Fiction. 2. Seasons-Fiction. Life cycles- Fiction] I. Title

First edition February 2017

The artwork was created with watercolor, airbrush and then digitally enhanced.

Dedicated to Chris and Erica

For Odelia and Simon

With heartfelt gratitude to
my husband Brett
and my dear friends
Julie and Robbie

Deep in a sleepy forest, a young little tree stood
surrounded by a group of great tall trees. Everyday, she
would bother the older trees with the same silly questions.

"Does it look like I've grown taller since this morning?"
and
"Do you think that the sun likes me best because my leaves look so shiny?"

The older trees rapidly grew tired of her vain and silly behavior.
They chose to ignore her constant questions.
This didn't really bother the little tree because she had other friends
who would pay attention to her...

like her good friends the wind and the birds. While the
birds sang their songs, she would sway, bend and flutter her
leaves in a graceful wind dance.

But her best friend was the caterpillar. He would visit everyday, and tell her the news of the forest. She looked forward to his visits most of all.

One day, the young tree noticed strange events happening around her. The days and nights were starting to get colder, and in the morning, she would notice something icy and glittery covering everything in the forest.

She also noticed that she and the taller trees were changing. The green leaves that filled her branches were turning crimson, yellow and orange.

However, the biggest change in the little tree's life was that her best friend the caterpillar had not been around for his daily visits.

"What's going on around here?!" she cried up to the sky.
One of the older trees took pity on her confusion and said, "It's Autumn
you foolish little tree. There's nothing to worry about. Your leaves will
change color, fall off and you'll go into a deep Winter sleep."

"FALL OFF?!" she shouted. "Not my leaves, maybe you'll lose your leaves, but I'm going to hold tightly onto mine!" And as she spoke these defiant words, one of her leaves delicately floated to the forest floor.

"This can't be! I can see it happening to them because they're so old, but I'm too young to go bald!" She shut her eyes and started to cry.

Days and weeks passed. More and more leaves fell from her branches.

She no longer wanted to dance with the birds and the wind.
All she wanted to do was cry and feel sorry for herself.

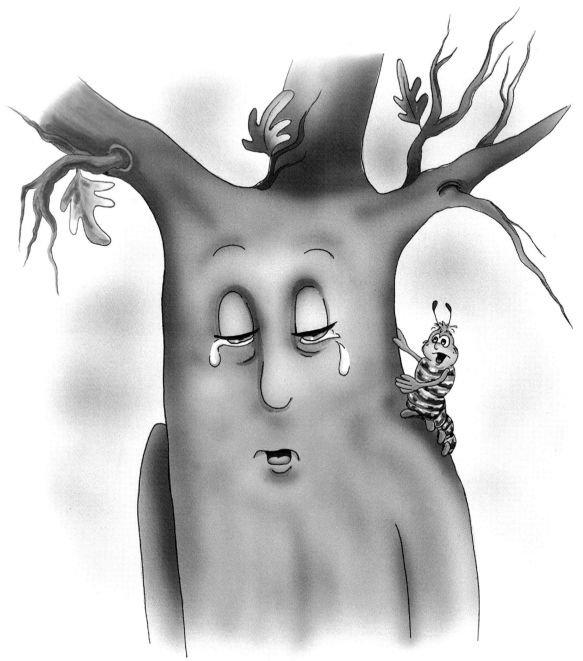

When she had almost given up hope, the caterpillar returned. "Where
have you been?" she asked in a sad quiet voice. The caterpillar noticed
how upset she was and said, "I've been busy getting ready for Winter.
What's wrong little tree?" "Well look at me... I'm balding!" she cried.

The caterpillar tried not to giggle and said, "You're not balding. You're just getting ready for your Winter sleep. Then in the Spring, you'll wake up with new green leaves." His words confused and comforted her at the same time. What was this Winter sleep that everyone was talking about?

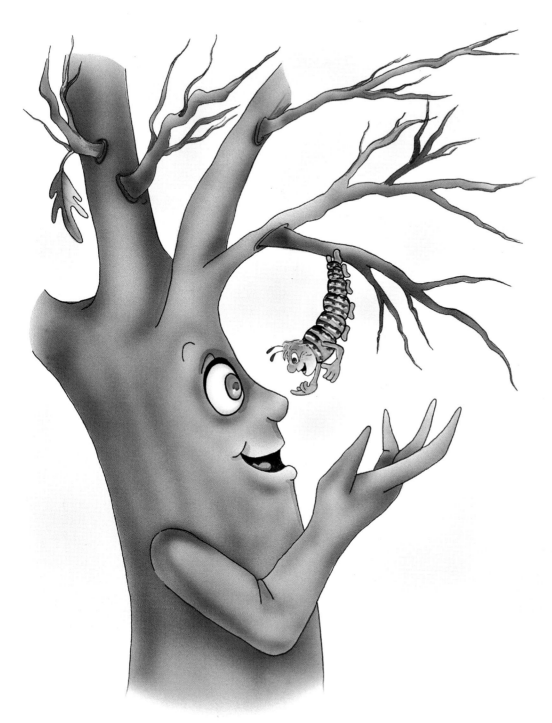

She gave him a puzzled look. "What about you?" she asked.
"I was going to make a cocoon and spend my Winter with you."

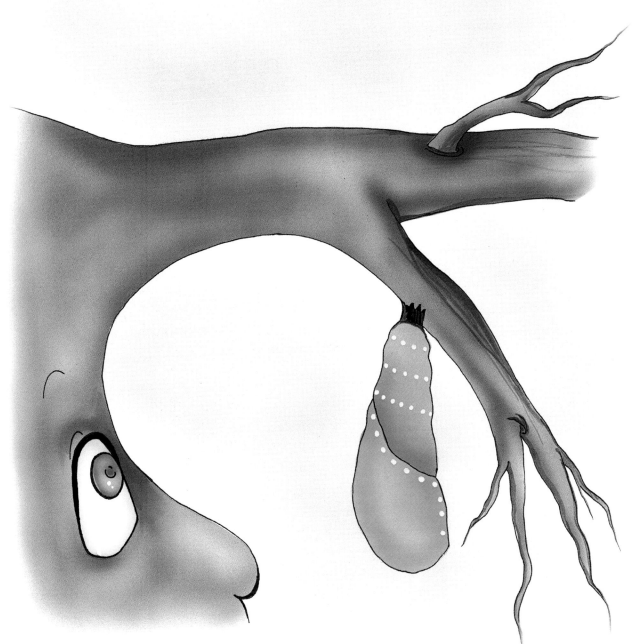

"Watch what I can do." he said. She looked on in amazement as he inched his way out onto one of her branches and began to spin a bright blue cocoon.

"Are you in there?" she whispered. "Yes little tree, I'm in here. Now let's shut our eyes and go to sleep." he said with a yawn.

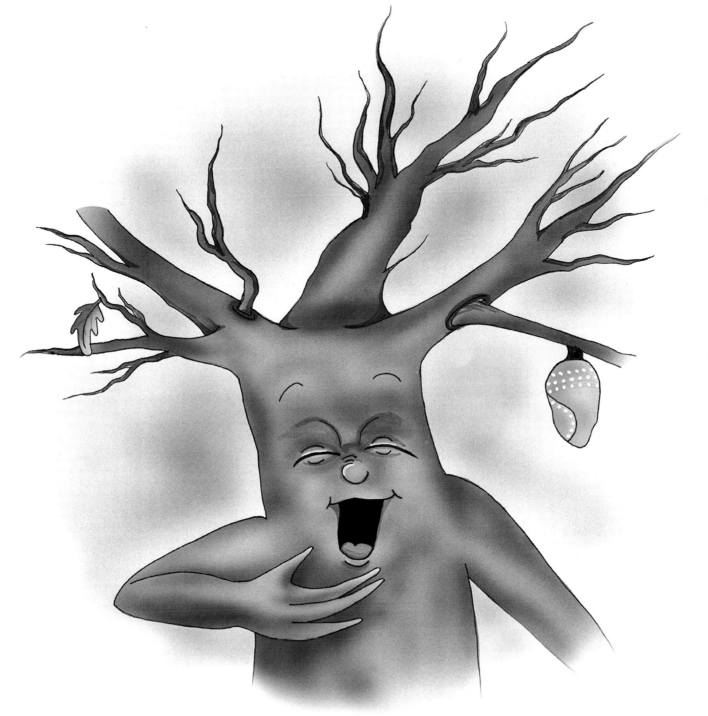

The young tree opened her mouth and
yawned a very sleepy yawn.

She shut her eyes and let
her last leaf fall.
A gentle snow began to drift
down over the
sleeping forest.
Autumn gave way to
Winter.

The cold snowy months slowly passed in the
forest until March came along.

The long Winter nights started to get shorter. The days started to grow longer. The snow melted away, and Spring finaly arrived with warmer weather.

The young tree stretched and slowly opened her eyes.
She looked up at the older trees. They weren't bare anymore!

Next, she looked down. The ground seemed a little further away.
Had she grown while she was asleep?

Now came the moment of truth. She took a deep breath
and carefully looked at her own branches. There she saw the lovely green
leaves that she thought were gone forever. The caterpillar had
been right. "It's about time you woke up little tree." said a familiar voice.

"Do I know you?" she asked.

"I'm the caterpillar. Don't you remember me?"

"Of course I remember the caterpillar, but you look so different." she said.
The butterfly explained that time and nature had a way of making things
change and grow, but that he was still the same caterpillar deep inside.

"Have I changed and grown?" she quietly asked.

"Yes," answered the butterfly, "you're wiser, taller
and even more beautiful than last year."

She breathed a sigh of relief and their smiles lit up the forest.
The little tree felt the wind flutter her leaves, and heard the birds singing her
favorite song. She looked at her friend the butterfly and said,
"Let's dance."